The Art of Ivy

From Pest to Pedestal

Martin R Thorne

Layout and presentation by Martin Roy Thorne

Plate 1

"Nothing is hurried, nothing takes too much time. Prised from its host the ivy is stripped, seasoned and shaped over long hours until its final form is decided.

The resultant sculpted ivy touches the senses. sinuous, sensual, vibrant, unique and serves to remind us of how beautiful nature really is............"

quote - Malcolm Victory (former mayor of Malvern)

Index

…...................

Plate 2   **Swan Lake**

Plate 3

INTRODUCTION

The artists love of trees was born out of a childhood spent amongst the ancient oaks and elms of south east England. Sadly most of the trees that martin grew up with have now gone to Dutch elm disease and urban development. This experience triggered in him a deep respect for the natural world, expressed by his work in, and care of , hedgerow and woodland.

Over the years this has combined with his fascination for curves and connectivity and led Martin to a unique and highly expressive art form.
His artistry in this medium is also inspired by the work of Salvador Dali .

Plate 4   **Alien rising**

Plate 5   **The Malvern hills**

Now working from a studio in Malvern, arguably the heart of England, the majestic Malvern hills loom large on the skyline, inspiring his work.

It is here, through a combination of artistic vision and skill, that the complex shapes of the ivy become exotic and evocative works of art.

Plate 6   circa 1996

Plate 7   **Ivy overgrowth**

THE ART OF IVY by Martin R Thorne.

A love of woodland and hedgerow has led me to an active interest in its maintenance, which I have undertaken, with approval from landowners, for over 25yrs.

My relationship with the countryside started at about the age of ten, where I would spend all my free time in solitary exploration of flaura and fauna .

As a teenager I witnessed the loss of swathes of mature English elms, stricken by dutch elm disease. I also witnessed the ungoverned clearance of large areas of ancient hedgerows to housing development.

These days mature trees are protected by planning laws and existing hedgerows also have to be considered in any new building project, we can be thankful for that !

It has become apparent to me, in England at least, that over the last 50yrs or so there has been a change in the management of hedgerows and brook sides. Further reductions in the rural labor force, changing attitudes in the rural population, the fact that coppicing and pollarding are no longer common practice, has seen an increase in the amount of hedgerows being allowed to grow out.

Plate 8

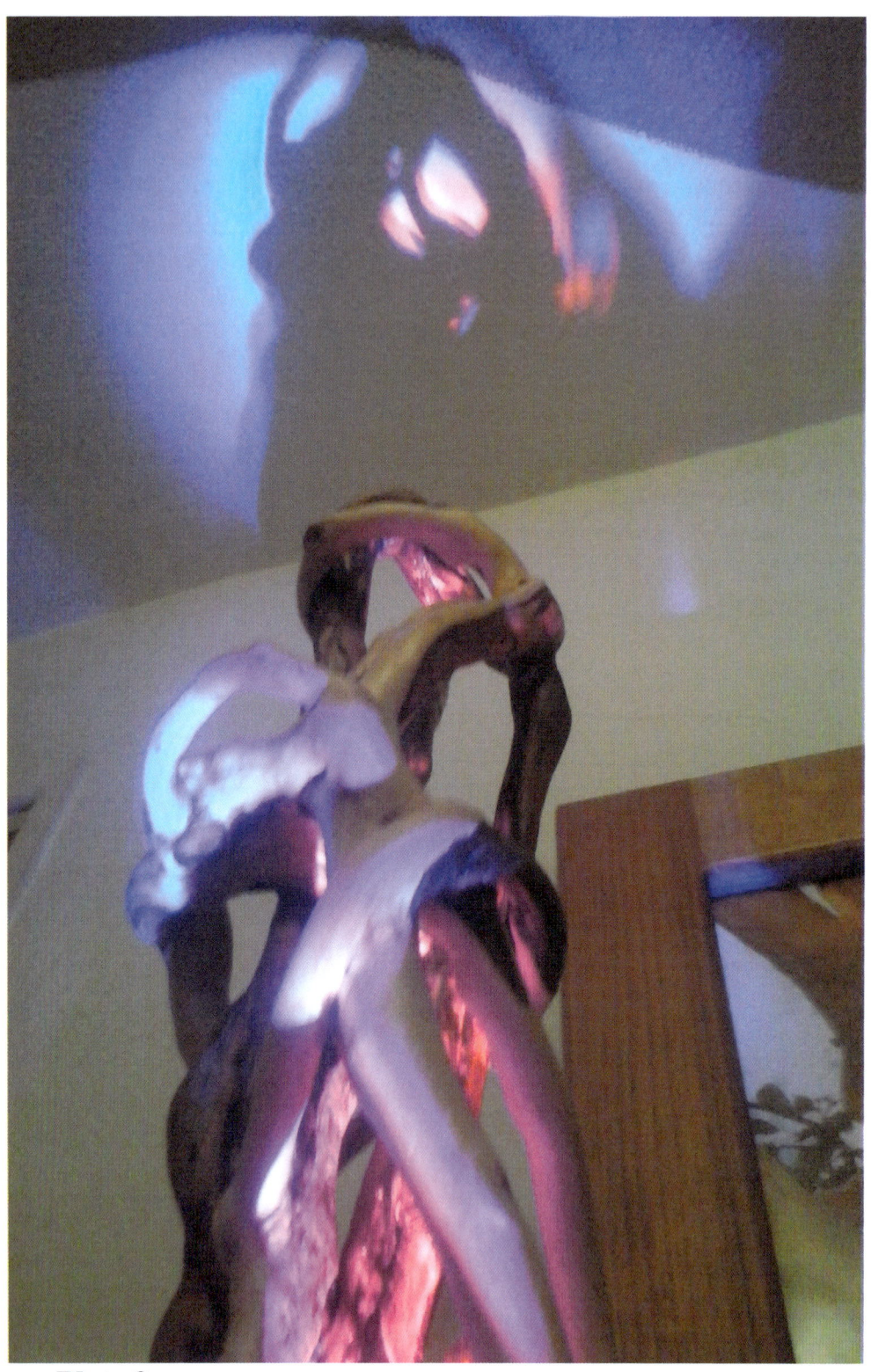

Plate 9

Plate 10   Saxon ditch

   This for the most part is not a bad thing, as many more trees of all kinds are being allowed to mature naturally and the hedgerow still maintains habitat and thoroughfare to a wide range of flora and fauna.

   There are some problems that have arisen with this approach, one of which is the control of ivy, uncontrolled growth brings an increase in the incidence of trees falling into the roadside and can lead to the breakdown of ancient hedgerow.

Plate 11

Plate 12

The increasing encroachment of human activity into the countryside makes it vitally important that we maintain and protect existing hedgerows and brooksides. This is necessary in order to balance that which we have unbalanced.

Changing climate also plays an increasingly damaging role, high winds occurring with greater frequency, and excessive rainfalls when deciduous trees are in full leaf.

All this increases the vulnerability of trees in exposed positions.

Plate 13   Vulnerable chestnut tree

Plate 14

One of the by products of hedgerow maintenance is discarded ivy, its artistic potential was not long in making itself known to me.

The shape and sensuality of ivy spoke of life form, morphism, connectivity and evolution of the mind as well as of life.

If my sculptures have an aim then it is that I hope to inspire a respect for nature and its creations, and to encourage others to work with nature not against it.

I hope this book serves to explain how and why ivy sometimes needs to be properly managed and also show how you can, through diligence with minimal tools, produce your own unique example of natures art.

Plate 17

ABOUT IVY

Hedera Helix, the common ivy, is a prominent plant in legend and lore, strongly associated with the god Bacchus and the brewing of beers.

In the middle ages its foliage was often hung upon a stake in order to indicate the presence of a tavern or drinking house.

In recent history the Victorians explored and named most of an estimated 500 varieties. Ivy is very disease resistant and can reach great age.

In Ginac, France there is a specimen reputed to be about 400 years old. The host tree has long since died away and the remaining ivy has been supported.

Ivy is often thought of as a destroyer of trees, but whilst slow growing small trees, thorn, damson and sloe for instance, can find its weight too great a burden, to healthy larger trees in the woodland, the ivy is merely a passenger.

Observable in winter as a wonderful rich green cloak, the ivy provides habitat to a rich variety of wildlife.

It is a hardwood and as with any tree, its age can be told by taking a cross-section and counting the rings.

•• ••••••••••••••••••••••••

Plate 18   It would be a crime to cut this venerable old ivy.

Plate 19

IVY OVERGROWTH

It is at the meeting points of human activity and the natural world that problems arise, infestation of bramble and nettle on unmanaged 'waste' land, encroachment of footpaths and byways by shrubs and tree growth and the spread of litter into the natural ecosystem.

Plate 20   **Stripping in progress**

Managing these points of friction requires the combined efforts of tree wardens, footpath wardens and conservation groups, also a host of volunteers from the community.

One problem at present largely overlooked, is the over growth of ivy in sunlight rich positions, such as roadsides and alongside footpaths where light can reach the entire length of trees and not just the top, as would be the case in woodland and forest.

Plate 21

This allows the ivy to grow vigorously up the sunlit side of trees . Isolated stands of small trees, such as sloe damson, blackthorn etc, are also being lost to the ivy.

This is a neglected but increasingly necessary part of hedgerow and treeline maintenance. It is a task that can easily be undertaken by footpath wardens and the like.

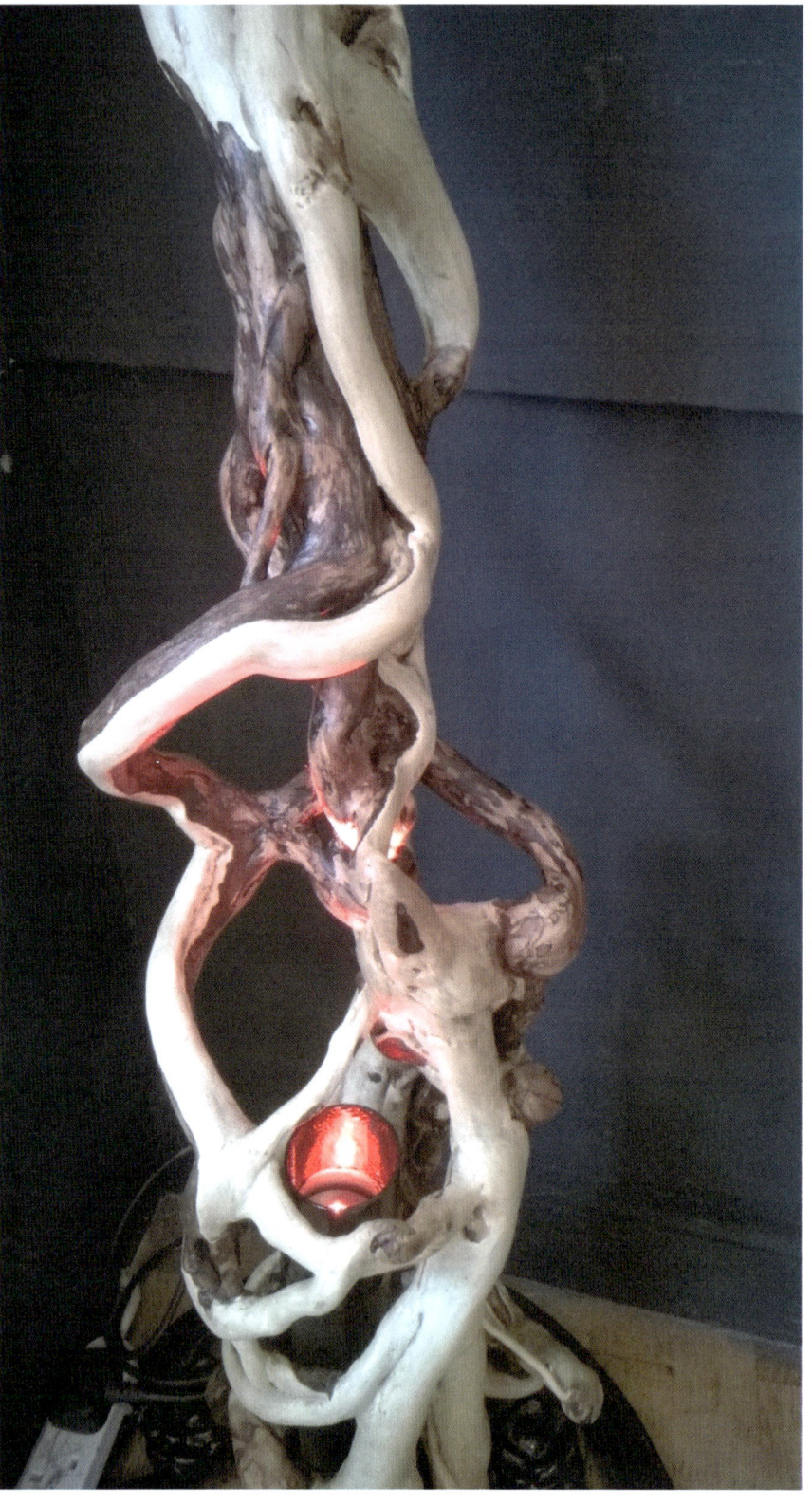

IVY CLEARANCE

Hedgerow maintenance covers a whole range of issues, ranging from simply cutting back brambles on a footpath right through to helping out in the long term preservation of scattered remnants of ancient woodlands and the hedgerows that link them up.

Plate 23

Some of this work requires cutting ivy from those trees in danger of being overwhelmed or being toppled across a fence, footpath or road.

Plate 24
    **Overladen ash trees with limbs falling to footpath,
prime candidates for ivy clearance.**

It is in the process of hedgerow and treeline husbandry that I occasionally acquire usable pieces of ivy that have sculptural possibilities.

Always work with the idea that nothing in nature is wrong, tidiness is a human concept, everything has its purpose in the ecosystem, its all about maintaining a balanced environment for all.

Never cut ivy without applying these guidelines,

The structural stability of its host tree,

Aesthetics as in when altering the view,

Balancing possible loss of wildlife habitat in the short term with sustaining habitat in the long term.

Last but most important, permission from the landowner.

Plate 26

Having decided that cutting of ivy is required there is the further decision on where and how to cut the ivy, there are three main approaches to this.

Full clearance.

This is when we cut all the ivy at ground level and cut all round at the bole or 1st major branch removing all the ivy from the trunk.

Plate 27   Plate 28

Plate 29

Burr Oak   partially cleared

Partial clearance.

This is where there are two or more branches of ivy running up the tree, here you can cut away some of the uprights leaving just one in place, this will reduce the weight and growth rate considerably whilst maintaining some habitat.

Topping out

This will involve leaving the ivy live on the trunk and cutting at the bole, cut a gap of at least six inches, to prevent re-connection.

This method will apply when the lower growth is mature and dynamic to look at. Ivy can live to a great age and as with any other old tree, preservation is always preferable.

…......................

Plate 30   Topped out

Plate 31

IVY IN THE GARDEN

    Many people use ivy as a screen or cover for archways the original intention of this is to present that classic hanging garden look, with long trails of ivy in the juvenile stage with triangular leaves.

    If left unmanaged the ivy is likely to switch to its adult form, becoming stiff and woody with oval leaves.

    In order to maintain the ivy in its juvenile form it is necessary to cut out any shoots that have started to change.
    Do this annually.

Plate 34

REMOVING IVY

Using examples illustrated we can go through the entire journey from saving a tree to producing a work of art.

Plate 35

As you can see illustrated, a mature hawthorn tree is leaning into the road being slowly toppled by the dense growth of ivy along its entire length.

This is not normal as for the most part ivy and trees will maintain a balance in the woodland.

Plate 36

This lopsided growth pattern is caused by the sunlight reaching one side of the tree via the roadway. In woodland the tree canopy would reduce the amount of sunlight available to the ivy.

In this example we can see that although habitat will be lost by cutting the ivy this preferable to losing the hawthorn.

Plate 37

Having removed the lower leaves the cause of leaning becomes apparent. The ivy has overlayed on itself and built up to quite a thickness on one side of the trunk, with the same tendency right up to the crown, this puts considerable stress on the host tree.

Plate 38

In most cases it is better to remove the ivy entirely from the bole as well as the trunk of the tree. Not only will that slow reinfestment but more importantly in the case of older pollarded trees, will allow proper inspection by tree surgeons.

It also enhances the look of the tree. The exceptions to this would be age of ivy (topping out) and habitat balance (partial clearance).

Plate 41   **The wizard**

This piece was torn from an old pollarded Oak.
Left to grow out, it succumbed to high winds.

Quite often ivy is controlled by simply nipping through the base of the ivy with a chainsaw, this approach has the potential to damage or scar the tree and it is very easy to miss smaller tendrils. The ability of the ivy to rapidly fuse to itself means that just a small shoot left to bridge the gap will sustain ivy above the cut.

Plate 42

Plate 43   **Early works**

The tools I use for this work are a standard handsaw, a flat lever, small hand axe and a pair of secateurs is always useful.

DO NOT USE a chainsaw or bow-saw.

A bow-saw is positively dangerous for this operation as they can bounce on the ivy and will jam quite frequently, you wouldn't want to tear your skin.

A chainsaw is also dangerous as you're working at awkward angles. It is also dangerous for the tree, all to easy to badly damage the bark.

Plate 44   Ivy ready to cut

Plate 45   Scorpio

First cut ivy at the bole or 1st major branch of the host tree, usually 1 ½ to 2 ½ metres, then cut the ivy at ground level.

The hand axe, you may need this to sever ivy at ground level.

Plate 46   Severing ivy

Plate 47   **Trunk cleared**

Sometimes the saw will jam as the ivy settles, if you feel this then withdraw saw and make a second cut about 5mm to one side. This will enable you to knock out the thin wedge and finish the cut.

Mostly the entire section of ivy can now be pulled off the host tree, but a large piece doesn't come off that easily, you'll need a strong lever and patience, being careful not to damage the host trees bark.

Hawthorn for instance although a very hardy species, its bark is surprisingly easy to tear.

Its worth noting that green ivy has some flexibility so with some care and patience it is possible to remove, in one piece, ivy that completely envelopes the host tree.

The handsaw, in my experience this is by far the best tool for cutting ivy, which is easy to cut when green, a handsaw also allows you to make awkwardly angled cuts relatively safely.

Practice sawing with both left and right hands, this will save you a lot of body movement and effort.

Remember to wear gloves, a spider bite can be nasty and the hedgerow can be very prickly, also you should wear a hat, not necessarily a hard-hat.

When working with ivy in the hedgerow and woodland there is lot of dry dusty material in the air. Wear a mask if you have an allergy.

Plate 48　　　　　　　**Tiffany style insets**

STRIPPING THE IVY

I have found that when working with freshly cut ivy it can get a bit heady, so some ventilation is advisable, I also suggest you hose down your piece of ivy to remove dust and loose material and the insects living on it.

You're advised to wear gloves as a matter of rule, in some situations it is advisable to use eye protection.

Plate 49   Half stripped

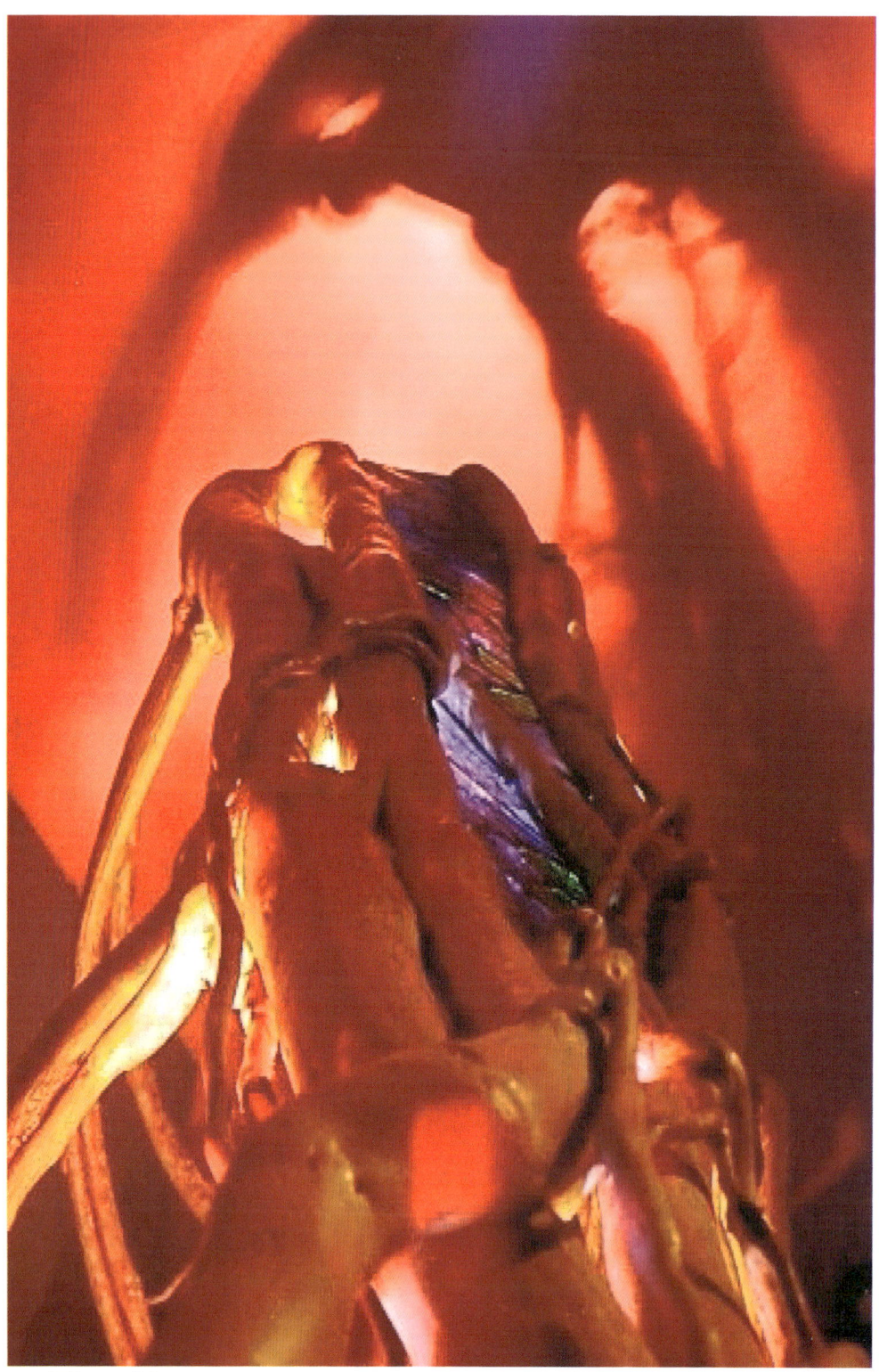

Plate 50

When stripping green ivy you have a few days to a week before it dries to a point where the bark has adhered to the underlying wood , if this happens you'll have to wait till the piece is fully dry then soak in water to soften the bark.

Plate 51   Stripping knives

Use a short knife, a cut down table knife will do nicely not too sharp otherwise you will be marking the underlying wood, start peeling of the bark, this is a fairly self evident process but time consuming, so start with a small piece.

As you strip the bark have by your side a small saw, I use a hacksaw blade, use this to remove odds and ends, broken sections and small branches that you don't want to keep. These cuts you will later be rubbing down with a rasp and sandpaper.

Plate 52

I again suggest that you would be well advised to practice using both hands, this will save continual moving of piece, it will seem awkward at first but persevere as this ability to move tools from hand to hand is useful anyway ,regardless of the task.

Plate 53   Strip complete

Its worth noting that ivy is a hard wood when dry, so it is advisable to work the wood whilst green removing unwanted stumps and roughly sculpting large cut ends with good sharp chisel and mallet.

Plate 54   **Hands on**

Plate 55   **A helping hand**

Plate 56

Bear in mind that there are variations of ivy and growing conditions that affect the heartwood, ranging from white and unblemished through to mottled and spiky. You never know what nature will give you for your efforts.

Having stripped most of the bark off your piece of ivy it will be looking rather messy, with bits of pith lodged in the nooks and crannies of the ivy.

Don't be put off it will all come good later.

Keep picking away at the residue of bark material using the hacksaw in combination with your knife, a jet wash is useful for occasionally clearing the loose debris.

....

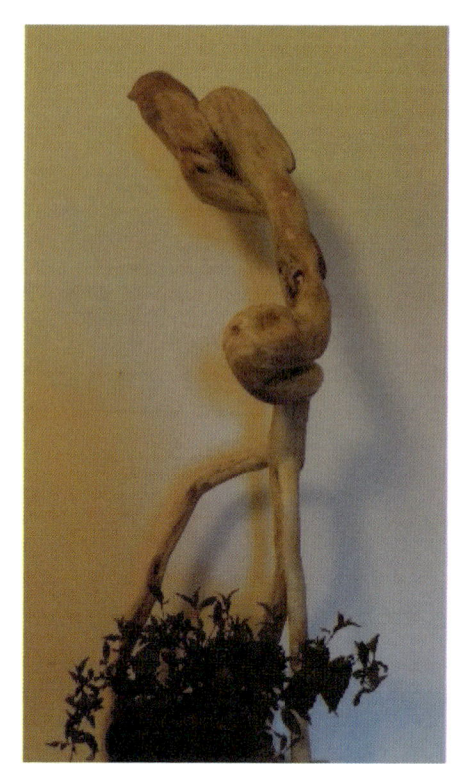

A NOTE ON TANNING

The bark of a tree contains tanning and if the ivy is left to dry before stripping the tanning will stain the ivy to a nutty brown.

If this finish is preferable then you would allow the ivy to dry completely and then soak the seasoned piece in water for several hours before using a hose or pressure washer to strip away the bark.   Occasionally assisting the removal of bark with the stripping knife.

Plate 58   **The Thinker**

Plate 59

DRYING/SEASONING

If the ivy has not already seasoned by the time you've finished stripping then store it in a dry place so as to avoid picking up mildew. I can't stress this enough, if you allow your fresh stripped ivy to stand in a damp or open air environment, the wood will almost certainly pick up what I call black eye mold. This mold gets into the pores of the wood and makes it look dirty, it is impossible to remove without damaging the heartwood surface, and makes the wood look dirty.

Store away from any direct source of heating, radiator, fire etc, in order to avoid excessive cracking.

Seasoning takes about 3-10 weeks according to thickness of ivy and the time of year. You will know when its dry because there is a considerable difference in weight, ivy is very rich in water when green.

Of course you will appreciate that experience counts for a lot, so I would advise that you to play around with some small bits and get used to this medium.

Plate 60   **Woodhenge at Eastnor castle**

Plate 61   **Play and Display**

SHAPING

This is the truly creative stage, you are now sculpting the ivy. Take your time, look at it for a few days, like most art it is not obvious where its going at first.

Do not be frightened of cutting bits off that slightly annoy the eye, a bit more space can actually add to the flow and shape.

Having shaped the ivy and removed all the bits you don't want you can now take a rasp to the cut ends and remove any sharp edges now rub those parts down with coarse sandpaper. Now rub down the entire surface with fine sandpaper removing all the roughness. NOTE -Use cloth backed sandpaper.

Plate 63   **Bishops ear**

Brush or wash down using a large paintbrush as this will get in all the crevices.

I have to emphasize that it is important to remove all those little bits of bark, it makes the difference between a good and a special finish.

If you have done the job properly you should be able to caress the ivy and feel the wood flowing beneath your hands.

Plate 64   Smoothed section

Plate 65

FINISHING

Now you should treat the wood with a clear anti fungal woodworm treatment. Apply with a small brush, wear glasses and gloves!!!!!!!!!!!!!

If your sculpture does not stand without support you might consider attaching a wooden base. One way to attach a piece of ivy to a block of wood or stump is to use dowel and water proof wood glue.

I generally use 6-10mm ramming. First apply glue to all contact points between ivy and block, support in place and allow to dry overnight.

Now drill 6mm holes in strategic positions, apply glue to dowels and insert, you may need to insert dowel with a few taps so as to fully locate. Once its dry rub down protruding dowels.

Plate 67   **Hawk**

Once glue and treatment has dried you can begin applying coats of oil, danish oil for instance, three coats would be minimum, rubbing down between applications.

A light rub down between coats will make for a better finish, once the oil is fully dry you may apply beeswax and then buff to a fabulous finish.

Note- if your piece is going in the garden or terrace Do Not use beeswax as rain water will discolor it.

Plate 68   Installation 2002

Plate 69

AFTERCARE

It is important to check for signs of woodworm at least once a year, if you should detect fresh holes in the wood acquire a suitable anti woodworm treatment and inject into holes, wait a few weeks for any residual infestation.

Once clear I suggest you fill the old holes with wax, this will make it easier to identify any recurrence in future

Plate 70   An artist and his dog

Plate 71   **Lightning damaged willow**

Plate 72

DIMORPHISM

    The Ivy has a juvenile form, that's the one you know of as a house plant, it has to go through a process known as dimorphism to reach adulthood.

    When this change happens the leaves change from the commonly known triangular shape to a more elliptical shape.

Plates 73/74   **Adult & juvenile foliage**

Plate 75

This change to adulthood occurs when the ivy reaches open sunlight ,as in the woodland canopy. It is at this point that ivy goes through the process of dimorphism becoming a tree in its own right.

The ivy needs support in order to reach the woodland canopy, it acts like clinging vine having aerial roots that form along the stems and cling to surfaces like tiny suction cups.

Its normal habitat is woodland where it spreads, in its juvenile form, as creeping ground cover.

It is NOT a parasite

Plate 76

Plate 77   **Scorpio**

DUTCH ELM DISEASE

This disease which comes in the form of a fungus is picked up by the elm bark beetle which then, unknowingly, spreads the disease .

Dead wood is an ideal breeding ground for the elm bark beetle, so dead elm should ideally be destroyed by burial or burning.   At the very least dead elm should be cut down, removed from the hedgerow and turned to firewood.

Regular cutting of elm to the hedge height helps a tree use its natural defenses against dutch elm disease, and reduces breeding and landing sites for the elm bark beetle.   If left to grow higher than the hedgerow the elm becomes extremely vulnerable to invasion by the beetle.

By doing this we can greatly reduce the chance of infection whilst also reducing the degree of infection carried in the wind. This increases the long term survival rates of our remaining mature specimens.

....

The up side is that In the long term disease resistant varieties will arise through the process of natural selection.

Also The elm spreads by send out lateral roots that send up suckers, this ensures a continual regeneration in the case of fire or disease damage.

....

Plate 78   **Cocoon**

BARK EXPLAINED

Most trees have a layer known as the cork cambium, which produces the cork, the tough outer layer of the tree. This outer layer is all that we usually see of the bark.

The outer cork protects the tree from the elements - from scorching by the sun or drying by wind.

It also helps to ward off fungi and the many insects and mammals that would otherwise take easy advantage of the sugar-rich sap or the wood that it surrounds.

A short way beneath the crusty outer surface of bark there is a layer called the cambium. Each growing season the cambium adds a new layer of cells to the sapwood (newer xylem), which it surrounds. The sapwood or newer xylem, transports minerals up the tree from the roots.

The heartwood or older xylem, is at the center of the tree. It is essentially made up of dead cells, and provides much of the strength of the tree.

Plate 80   **Healthy hedgerow**

The artists past

As well as being sculptor, Martin is also a designer, an example of which is the Thorne & Mason lapslide, of which he is the co-inventor/designer.

He is also a musician and songwriter as shown in his albums and improvisation projects with other musicians, working under the name of 'Martin Thorne & Company'.

As a young man he worked as a technician involved with innovations such as, bar code technology, flight simulators, the London flood barrier.

A later period saw him spend 10yrs restoring leaded lights, learning this from a master of the trade, Malcolm Wytcherley one of the top exponents of this medieval skill.

► Mike Pryce meets a man who sculpts in ivy

Clinging to his craft. . .

THEY might just look like wiggly bits of wood to you, but beauty is in the eye of the beholder, so they say, and Martin Thorne has definitely got some inner vision.

Enough, anyway, to turn straggly lengths of ivy into sitting room conversation pieces... Almost surreal examples of artwork that can be used as plant pedestals, ornament stands, containers or just as decorations in their own right.

As far as he knows, he is the only person in the country at it and whenever he exhibits at local shows there is invariably a fascinated crowd wondering just what it's all about.

Martin looks the part too. — Sort of a cross between being left over from Woodstock and an environmental burrower beneath proposed bypass routes, he would be at home around the flickering campfire with his guitar.

In fact, he was

▲ 'I've a way with ivy.' Martin Thorne at work.

◄ Two examples of

► Martin Thorne relaxes on a sculpted seat with his pet Lassie.

away"

Plate 81   Evening news 1997

**Plate 82
Cafe Bliss
Worcester Arts Workshop**

Contact your local authority or parish council if you are interested in being a footpath or tree warden.

………........................

If you'd like to join a group activity then you could contact your local countryside centre, arts centre or woodland trust.

………........................

postscript

**I would like to thank family and friends
for their support in this project.
Martin R Thorne**

Printed in Great Britain
by Amazon